THE AMERICAN POETRY REVIEW /
HONICKMAN FIRST BOOK PRIZE

The Honickman Foundation is dedicated to the support of projects that promote spiritual growth and creativity, education and social change. At the heart of the mission of the Honickman Foundation is the belief that creativity enriches contemporary society because the arts are powerful tools for enlightenment, equity and empowerment, and must be encouraged to effect social change as well as personal growth. A current focus is on the particular power of photography and poetry to reflect and interpret reality, and, hence, to illuminate all that is true.

The annual American Poetry Review / Honickman First Book Prize offers publication of a book of poems, a $3,000 award, and distribution by Copper Canyon Press through Consortium. Each year a distinguished poet is chosen to judge the prize and write an introduction to the winning book. The purpose of the prize is to encourage excellence in poetry, and to provide a wide readership for a deserving first book of poems. *Paraph of Bone & Other Kinds of Blue* is the fourth book in the series.

Paraph of Bone
& Other Kinds of Blue

Winners of The American Poetry Review / Honickman First Book Prize

 ⸘

Joshua Beckman *Things Are Happening* *1998*

Dana Levin *In the Surgical Theatre* *1999*

Anne Marie Macari *Ivory Cradle* *2000*

Ed Pavlić *Paraph of Bone & Other Kinds of Blue* *2001*

Paraph of Bone & Other Kinds of Blue

Poems

Ed Pavlić

Winner of The APR / Honickman First Book Prize

The American Poetry Review ⚬ *Philadelphia*

Distribution by Copper Canyon Press / Consortium.

Library of Congress Catalogue Card Number: 2001132035

ISBN 0-9663395-7-6 (cloth, alk. paper)
ISBN 0-9663395-8-4 (pbk., alk. paper)

First edition
Designed by Adrianne Onderdonk Dudden
Composed by Duke & Company

Thanks to the editors of the following magazines, where some of the poems in this book first appeared: Indiana Review, Open City, DoubleTake, Colorado Review, Cross Connect, The Cortland Review, Black Warrior Review, A Gathering of the Tribes, *and* The American Poetry Review.

The author wishes to express his gratitude to the Provincetown Fine Arts Work Center and the Vermont Studio Center for the space they provided during the writing and revising of this book. Added thanks to the many, many people who read and/or listened to various pieces of the puzzle over the past few years: Donia Allen, Trudi Witonsky, Craig Werner, Jordan Smith, Ariel Torsone, Crystal Williams, Michael Ladd, Adrian Frazier, Yusef Komunyakaa, Jonathan Shapiro, Eric Lassitter, Harry Marten, Jim McCord, Andrew Krivak, Bonney MacDonald, Norman Dubie, and Adrienne Rich.

For Stacey, Milan, and Sunčana

Contents

Foreword

by Adrienne Rich

It is not always true, anywhere, that artistic originality and integrity
will be recognized. In a deeply riven society it is not necessarily true that
judges—whether of the Supreme Court variety or for poetry prizes—
will possess both competence and integrity to rule on the materials
before them.

Disclaimer: "Judging" a literary, let alone a poetic, prize becomes the
more difficult as you try to recognize competing claims and give honor-
able consideration to work you might in a different context merely
have skimmed. You stretch yourself, check on yourself. You finger many
strands in many poetries, since American poetry is no one thing. In this
process, and from among many manuscripts, Ed Pavlić's *Paraph of Bone
& Other Kinds of Blue* emerged as a mature, integrated presence, a voice
of passionate intelligence.

In other manuscripts I found literary fluency, programmatic despair,
imitations of recent stylistic experiments, verbosity, lurid hyperbole,
juvenile self-pity, touristic exotica, some wit, a narcissism of family
revelations. Overall disappointing in many of the collections was an
absence of poetic/emotional conviction, as if no self-creating, self-
critical personality had conceived them. I feared many were the uncon-
structed, hopefully marketable, contents of MFA portfolios. I kept
wondering why—in this group of younger poets—obeisance to intel-
lectual constructs seemed to displace natural energy, the charged,
intensely changing conversation of poet and world.

To have found Ed Pavlić's *Paraph of Bone & Other Kinds of Blue* gave
this judge an infusion of hope. It's a fully conceived book, speaking
as a whole from the first lines to the last. What is in here belongs here,
and what is in here is consciously shaped. Mr. Pavlić has listened closely
to our most profound American art, the blues and jazz, and that music
has not only helped him achieve poetic form but allowed him to explore
a mesh of experience extraneous to literary theories. He is, doubtless,
aware of such theories, but the voices in his poems flow from a denser
space, having penetrated a denser reality, returning via the imagination
and its many discontents. In many of them, music and its creation/per-

formance are metaphorized into human relationships. This is intimate and soulful work, breathing, brushing, or tonguing its instrument.

The music evoked within this book is transcendent in its reaches. Jazz and the blues have infused all the arts with elements of improvisation and risk which may be copycatted but never formulated. To his engagement with this tradition Ed Pavlić adds an erotics of language, vernacular or mysterious. I looked up *paraph, nidi, isatine, raphe,* in Webster's and found myself aware, yet again, that there are words for things we barely acknowledge, yet people have used them, the words are there. There is no showy erudition in Pavlić's use of such words: they are an extension of poetry.

These are some of the kinds of lines a judge might catch on to and say: Someone has actually *been* here:

a brand burned into naked wood   Property of PS 129
  an old-time upright wheeled out to the playground
    paradiddle & round the back   hand clap

& tight coil rhythm bounce   eyes closed   smoke stained
  finger tips tangent to ivory   sunshine in a wide-open mouth
    light poured like syrup   fast twitch reflex & cold

      trust   an amber lyric   between blurry
        strangers

                                          ("Spheres")

Don't sing it
  to me. Or I'll stay under
    here motionless

& blue-gilled. I'll drift
   away from the shattered place
      of irruption.

Where the summer song
   crossed the winter street,
      the corner

where we met. & don't
   worry about me,
      I'll stick close

to pockets of air beneath
   the surface. Snatch shallow
      breaths of marrow

from bends in the death-blue
   shoulder blade of the ice patch.
      Go on & sing it,

just not to me. Last night,
   for a moment at rest
      on the keys,

I saw my finger tips melt
   chord prints into your frozen
      back. & Gershwin's

limo didn't come around
   to keep us honest. . . .

("Isatine Blues")

Ed Pavlić, in his mid-thirties, has made a complex and beautiful first book. He must and will go further, because he can. It's a judge's pleasure to be able to point such a book toward the readers it deserves and who deserve it.

Adrienne Rich
January 2001

Anyone who doesn't
Tremble
At the gates
Of reality
Will be broken
By what they encounter
In the city

Paraph of Bone
   Other Kinds of Blue

Masqualéro

—after Miles

There's plenty that think we're twins. By 18
   we'd both wished secretly that it was true,
      & that it wasn't. Since we were 9

we met here on stealth banks of August,
   each year another Savior & sweet thanks be
      to Jesus for that old rowboat.

Remember my instructions when we met?
   I'd bent a coffee can into a scoop to hunt
      the mud banks for crawfish. "The whole

trick with blue pinchers is getting in behind
   without setting off a stir on their tail." Now
      we're getting to be His age. But apart

from watches & sky dates, you know how to find me
   when my head's full of scuppernong blossoms.
      So we cast off past wisteria

& into night silk beyond the river's edge. Empty skins
   of tree snakes, ash vibrissa, draw the canopy.
      Tangles of moss wisp past my cheeks,

fall out of a lullaby. No moon. If I spark my lighter,
   willows young & old pretend they don't breathe
      the dark, don't slip thru nights

in tangos with cypress & Saturn tuned in to bent
   underwater reeds. Posed they stand like a big-city
      crowd at a bus stop, & just reach

off the bank for elbow room. Come out that white blouse
   & upside down, you watch open lilies fall away,
      a bird's eye vision

of your daddy's parachute into the Mekong Delta.
   A back bend arched over the bow, your bare torso slips
      thru a summer breeze, cuts

a hush in the cicada din. A pale gash torn past my lips
   leaves the night open. Light-plays off my chrome
      Zippo. Hershey's kisses harden

into rose thorns dense as a shut eye's faith in Tarot.
   My name, dry salt on an arch-smooth eyebrow,
      vanishes into steamed woods & gut-heavy

air like sweat into a prayer for rain. We take on water
   in each Decatur Street groan for Mercy. It's far too late,
      slipway a damned sight too steep

for Esperanto or one-eyed jacks. To pull the moon
   back with cracked oars curved like tusks, you'd better
      mean it. It's about time for round two.

Oceanus descends with an acetylene tear & dreams
   of a blue tip, a cool flame; the other eye's been gone
      for years, blind & lid turned cold side out.

Imbroglio & Cuadrilla

Close your eyes & touch the nearest
   wet thing. There's no map to the next
      warm spot in the room,

no navel to watch so you can't be had
   by a quick pearl
      in the dark. Accidental then?

The legion of sorts
   that gather to a slumped beast,
      felled by picadors' letting. They'll find

vibrations can't be pillaged,
   or held hostage with hosannas. No mantra
      to tame the thing

that rides & lets ride. Were you handed the Eucharist
   under the table? Can you undress, slowly,
      down to your voice in the dark

just before we met? When fingers slipped & grace
   unbuttoned, winded trees hushed & clouds brought
      what we let fall.

Sacred Rum Toes

On Sundays, dips her feet
   in Barbancourt & gray with newsprint
     ash,

give me the news baby, just the news —
   patrols the block for windburned
     saints. Be

cause every week's a best of seven
   & even with Mingus on Wednesday
     Night,

it always comes down three-three.
   Cursed God for a rained
     out Yankee

game. She meant it. Nonchalance coiled
   in her wrist, told Jehovah, Buddha, & the rest
     of the comments on the stoop

to *Step, I'm the wrong verse of Blakey's,*
   because no you don't know what it is,
     to tear asunder.

}

She'd be a terrific murderer.
   One hand figured itself grown
      when her mother

died. Now, needle fingers fold
   precision in on nuance & modal tips
      lift

what you didn't, did you? even know
   was pain —like the black feather theft
      in death.

Her touch drips steely weight
   & runs down heavy like mercury
      beads. Then falls

away to regain its shape. A cat eye
   forms. Spheres of molten glass spin
      thru the marbler's

shaft. & gone to silence at the bottom
   of the pool. Rhythms, strings of the nidi
      travel thru bone

& in flesh waves without a goose
   ripple in my skin. She's the crowd
      I'm lost in.

We're keenly matched, a straight
   razor & a pearl;
      singular

on her walk back from the El
   as the nightly brick she carries
     home.

Confessions of a Piano Roll Lover

Pianola or not,
   memory's getting to be a crowded
     room. Forget

the door, but mindful of the hinge.
   Outside, frozen insides times pi,
     full of starlight

voices come in one eye & out
   the other. Watch who you're with,
     what holds you

together on steps between streetlights
   when shadows simmer & boil over.
     Outside-in looks

inside-out thru a spy-glass bottom
   of a shot of whiskey. Water flees into
     air trapped in

the iced surface of an upright's mirror.
   Here on the sandbank stool
     of a glass-made

torrent, I can smell sulphur & see
   the silver-green pool in a Steamboat
     stream that took

my sister's breath away. Even with tone
   & touch unhinged, hidden-out, &
     fallen in over

their heads, sure as pig-tails float,
   I know anything that clear is deeper
     than it sounds.

{

If the face I see in the mirror
   is more yours than mine,
      why do my hands

ache when they slide between
   your legs? Your breath in my mouth,
      steamed cognac

blown off an ice cube.
   If you'd get from behind me,
      I'd follow this

hush anywhere. Instead,
   you're what happens to suede
      shoes on

a walk to the beach at dawn.
   Or when, in the mist of a sky
      gone to night,

a flock of blackbirds turn
   on the red-winged
      pulse

of a thought & make for
   a glow at the bottom
      of the bay.

＄

A fever's drawn
  out this way. The deep touch
    recedes.

Nothing's right. Splintered
  scales & rotten staircases.
    Borrowed keys

& stolen fingers on the lamb,
  a kleptomaniac
    silk-fiend

runs thru a top drawer. Stomps
  on the pedal, dares the wire
    to uncoil. Turns

a pirouette of stillness sharp
  as the newly broken edge of an eye
    tooth & out

a bedroom window. No way to muffle
  it with a strong finish. I hold my throat
    to hum your name

in church & find what moves
  thru the lacquered grain, loud as shattered
    stained glass, soft

as Wednesday ash. Light & a roustabout
  scent of bayou steam risen
    thru the wood.

〈

The last player held himself
    prisoner with a kitchen knife
        in a dressing room

mirror. Said "first of you three that moves,
    none go on," not without altered fingerings
        matched to a lazy

left eye. Walked a tightrope, mainlined
    a gyroscope, scratched out changes
        & everything

else that goes down as dice kick
    up on the curb. Inhaling whatever's
        in the air tonight,

charted losses between metabolic thirst
    & the taste of sweat. Paralyzed
        by that mute

flash, God-kissed white-out
    that keeps generations from fucking
        each other

up too bad. Kept claiming it all
    had to do with "Catfish Blues" & that hook
        his daddy swallowed.

≀

& this new player,
   he's just a boy. Well
      drilled,

won't allow his thumb
   to drag behind his
      index

finger. Mistakes won't leave
   exit wounds, or
      bloom

in his lapel until
   they're his alone. Grown.
      With a pocket full

of rock salt
   in his gait, & jalapeño
      beard.

≀

I can't play the roll
　　anymore. A burned bridge
　　　or a dancer's

stretch. The bench creaks
　　as I rise, fingers reach past
　　　cracked

knuckles into a parable spin,
　　concentric eyes in a funnel cloud.
　　　Aches like Nijinski

curled up in sickled veins. When
　　I play & you dance, I fall where
　　　one mirror faces

another. *Myself When I'm Real*
　　& *All the Things You Are* on two turntables,
　　　four hands of angel glow

hover in & out of view. A glimpse of Morpho
　　dusted for flight & carried away
　　　on blue-eyed wings.

}

A spring rises at the speed of light
   & a sea turtle drops into an
      infinite well.

The age of light happens once. &
   the turtle flies forever, but dies thirsty.
      & still you move

in afternoon shade come down
   out of a willow. No matter
      the pyramid

or Pegasus Thales rode to the ship.
   I can hold an hour glass
      in one hand

& with the other, you prove a span
   in sight over land is liquid
      & direction

in sound under water invalid.
   All logarithmic hopes out-stripped,
      at sundown,

your shadow touches the east
   & a million night fingers crawl
      thru me in the lawn.

꿈

I could get back
  on the stool, but you know
    how I am

with directions. Have we been here
  before? You going in
    circles

with the world & me listening
  to myself listen. Remember
    the night

we met? You told me the Gospel
  of First Impressions & that
    my face was

too far away to touch; you took in
  my breath & vanished into
    sky blue sheets.

Communiqué, from on High

Remember the faces in the woodwork
   you laughed at when the light was on?
      Don't call me

for just any flash of heat in the dark. Save me.
   Thank me for the straight down sound
      in the rain. Beg me

for the hiss that moves an eye-tooth down
   to catch the wet vein in your neck. Remember
      our little time

of promises, on the shortcut from work
   you knew better than to take? Remember,
      there's no voice

that's not heard. The next time you sift thoughts
   to elude the mix & tone of the day, remember
      the crowd

you don't see. Call to me, hidden in the tangle
   of corpses down the hallway. Next time
      you go from light

to dark, you might need the secret note
   written in shadow quill, the cold bloom
      of essence encrypted

in your torso. Say the word, I'm on you
   like your mama's best
      & only friend.

Is It a Crime?

This may come. This may come
as some surprise.
                    —*Sade*

If the house is rigged
    & dark as a winter afternoon
        save a naked

bulb in the front closet
    & a wooden match struck
        in the attic.

If it took me all day,
    eleven mirrors, & close
        to a full roll

of duct tape. If I used far
    too many nails & our
        deposit is

sealed regret, plus
    interest. Like the times
        in the closet

with my grandmom's bread
    knife. Nose open, veins in my arm
        singing along

with serrations in the blade,
    the night I threw away
        half of one

in every pair of shoes
    you own. If I sit
        in a corner

of the attic & wait
    for you to come thru
        the door. If

another match sparks.
   Twelve of my faces flash
      & zigzag thru

the house. One floats
   amid shadows in the hallway.
      If, at each step,

you place the image
   & chart the ricochet.
      Arms opened,

reach for the wall
   on either side. Or light up
      & blow

smoke into your path.
   If you walk thru an unseen
      beam & my face

moves over yours.
   Might as well wear these
      blindfolds. Your lips

come apart & my eyes slip
   inside your mouth.
      You on tip-

toes at the bottom of the attic
   steps & me fresh out
      of matches.

Eyes closed, twelve
   faces stare in from under
      your lids. If,

in a sudden breath,
   you fall thru me hard, blown
      like April

snow thru gaunt limbs in a forest.
   If you touch my face &
      there's nothing

like sound in the room.
   If you follow the curve
      of the rail

up the stairway like my finger
   in the dark, down the maple slope
      of your hip.

You Sound Unseen

—for Phyllis Hyman

A red spot burns
   a cyclone on the cymbal's
     crown. Take

the night off. Give up
   the scar between
     hindsight &

the unheard. Save
   your ears for tongue-tips
     & the things

they do well. Let's
   don't disturb twisters
     of unspoken

brass. Leave sweat
   profiles alone on the
     sheet. Step

thru tastes & stain
   in the street. & nobody
     knows what

to do at the lakefront after
   a storm. Confessions wash
     ashore. Wave set

upon wave, knee deep
   in driftwood tangled & smooth
     as hammer

handles or ankle bones.
   & holding on means fingers
     hurt,

means we
braid our own
hair.

{

The El sickles thru.
　　Sparks shriek. Then glow
　　　in a low pulse-

ache. Shoves a grudge thru
　　tight veins toward missing limbs.
　　　At night,

if I smell tobacco in the breeze,
　　I can still feel my granddad's
　　　knotted hand

tuck me in bed, the firm
　　press of his Y shaped grip.
　　　Not a sound

from his ironworker's stride.
　　He told me about cold jobs.
　　　& high jobs

up in the Loop that floated blue
　　on morning fog blown in
　　　off the lake.

Said by 3:30, he could walk
　　a beam of light thru a smoky
　　　room for a shot

& a beer. Said the beauty
　　of an open coke furnace was
　　　you always knew

how much fire your chest
     could hold, & exactly where
          the Devil was.

{

An old man
   mutters into his drink,
     scalp silvered

ebony, dusted
   by a three day old
     shave.

Sits alone at the end
   of the bar. A carnation
     in his green

lapel. By '87, you'd already
   begun to whistle thru
     a few verses

of "Old Friend." Not fooled
   by the sequin sheen,
     wags

a missing index finger
   when a mic-swipe cleaves
     your voice.

Whispers under breath into
   the rift   *I know your*
     tricks now—

From across the room,
   a waitress sees him shake
     his fist

while candle-lit couples hold
   hands at tables up front.
      He lights

a cigarette & blows a cloud
   over his glassy-eyed
      scotch.

The cold traps
   a curl of smoke in the glass.
      A long ash

falls to the bar. Toasts
   touché   to the whistler
      & downs

the rest. With a wince,
   slides off the stool thru a red
      cloud behind

your silhouette & *Welcome to
   George's* frost-etched
      in the bar

mirror. Turns to go, reads
   his own lips   *Punish it woman,
      punish it.*

Wanted: Thief

[salary commensurate with experience]

I reach down to lift the diamond chip away
   from the frayed orange & black edge of the album
      label. It's been over

for years. Against an even rhythm of static, echoes
   of Oliver Nelson hiding time in his pocket,
      sleight of hand to mouth

lined with plush blue velvet from his saxophone
   case. But that isn't my memory. Arrived too late to have
      happened before I was born.

In the static I can hear hushed voices, boys on a bus.
   Rhythms of secrets & strategy. After the game,
      how best to palm purple

& green Now & Laters at the corner store. The needle's up,
   the scratch-rhythm goes double-time, dry-gasps
      of the thirsty cry.

In my sleep I touch sounds that glow & snap
   like white tungsten strands. I can feel a storm miles off,
      two potato sacks

rolled over in the trunk of my mom's new Rambler.
   It pulls me into a driveway, heavy thumps & falsetto
      hoots of my son's

bad bear dreams. On scribbled Crayola legs, a fugitive
   from the fridge door stumbles toward the sound that shoots
      thru his veins.

There you sit arrow straight, like your Uncle James
    driving a team under a Tidewater fire-flaught. Eyes like fists
        draped in ninon, drops

of moonlight squeeze out thru clenched fingers. Head
    matted in a wet tussle, you still hug the rescue squad with
        all fours. I picked you out of a tree-top

dipped in a salmon-blue tumble of bear claws, mirror
    to a crescent moon named just yesterday in an urgent warning
        to the world, *E-moom-dheer*.

If you see your breath, you can talk with the moon. Here,
    we sit in a fluent room & watch reddened whispers churn
        in a deep blue bed of coals.

A slow burn crawled thru its every fibre during the night.
    The lattice of the anchor log kept its shape, it weighs close
        to nothing. Like a stolen handful

of now, or someone else's music, nothing that light can be touched
    again. An easy push of year-old bellows, brown eyes
        in my lap aflame.

A orange glow from inside the log, flakes waft like trout gills
    in a blue stream of smoke & I can't tell an ash limb
        from wood that breathes.

Full Blown

that thing he strapped on
  was alive   a torn aorta   sun spots
    & arcs in a

magnetic fog   when he wakes
  off shore   Procyon hovers
    & waits for Sirius

to show   after ten minutes
  they can't talk
    over it

after thirty   they can't see
  thru it   the crowd just
    wants it

to go away   their heads wag
  they moan   a guffaw
    lips move

but they don't hear themselves
  everyone leaves   backs
    slumped   waves

roll past a flailing
  man on their way out
    to shore

a waitress tips out three ways:
  nada nada de nada   bar
    tender's hot

don't nobody drink from
  the blue rail of darkness
    hours

later   from behind
    dark shades   he whispers
        into the mic

long dead   we like
    to call that one
        Unity

Spring Run Off

With the first real sun,
   the flow gains force. In rivers
     of fugitives,

a hollow cheek flows past
   generations ago.
     Once, a whole

face appeared to the surface
   as if for breath. They nod & bump,
     cross borders

from midnight to being
   like barrels of prohibition whiskey
     caught in a Columbia

River eddy. Deadman's Eddy,
   named for a John Doe six-khaki
     bootlegger,

or a unionist who jumped in
   on the run from a Mounty. Already
     part crystal,

how can I measure the fear
   of the river & the howl of the lattice?
     As passages ebb,

lives are priced, named. Names
   mis-spelled, or lost. Death shifts
     the sands & the river

bank vanishes. Too late by the time
   teachers & sand-baggers arrived,
     I'd flooded the floor

with the faces of strangers. If profiles
    let go of names, hold
        both my hands

in the rain. If features scatter down
    the street like November leaves
        in a thunderstorm,

tell him now who his father
    was. A thumbnail Matisse
        runs down

the mirror, my face slips past
    in a pair of curves. It's beyond club
        chants & boys

& girls, come join the pastiche, a half-tone
    in the leaden walk of an unplayable
        song. If she's the hitch

in the metronome, I'm the age
    of the mirror. I remember
        the day

the cat lost the green out of its eyes. All
    summer, translucent nights
        shimmered thru

that room. We laughed, suddenly we
    could see the sable cat move
        against the velvet

ripples of darkness; but he couldn't see us.
    Hence the phrase from 1970 & the
        famous game on our

block: "a summer cat's bluff." For the rest
  of its life, even in the daytime,
    the cat stayed clear

of that night-blind room. & today,
  plush green won't sit still on
    the piano stool cushion.

Bedtime Stories by Roberta Flack

—For Madeline Wirtz

8:30's too early to sleep, when trees still stoop to the windows.
  The bad man, with big eyes & the evil cap might come tonight
    & not disappear when I open my eyes.

Even if it rains hard. I might even trade thunder & lightning
  if he'd stay away. From 8:30 to ten, I stay as near to the voices
    but out of sight just beyond the corner

on the stairs as I can. Unless dad's home. Then it's all too risky. But
  tonight he's on the road. I know. I heard mom talking to him
    on the phone,

about where my sister might be & how 13's too young to—
  "Just too young." Glared at me talking to him, she said "no fear,
    no brains." Mom always talks

about Dansville, Bradenton, Muncie, Pittsburgh, Williamsburg. Towns
  I know by name cause that's his job. My dad doesn't talk. He works.
    Other kids think my mom's divorced,

I tell them that my dad works. They say theirs does too. Except the ones
  whose moms are young, almost more like my sister Mary than my mom.
    Their dads are in Vietnam.

That's a war. I think it's about water. There's a big dam, men
  in a room come on all three channels at once & talk about the big
    dam in Washington. I think they call

the war in Vietnam Watergate. Once, in Montana, I saw Crazy Horse
  Dam. I remembered where it was for school, so I'd know. But now
    close, just around the corner,

at the top of the stairs. I know it's 9:00 cause I hear the spooky music.
  Night Gallery. It makes me think about how our cat sneaks through
    the yard after birds. Our neighbors

love birds. They tied a bell around our cat's neck. But she still runs
   thru the quiet dark in the yard & that bell doesn't ring.
      My sister's scared

when the cat's under her bed. I'm scared when she slips thru
   the silence of the dark like the man in my dreams. & I can't listen
      to the radio, not at night. Cause

there's a dying woman singing about a soft man. He's killing her
   & her voice haunts my ears, makes them hot, like coming inside
      in the winter if I didn't wear a hat,

like they're being stuck with pins. It's over a mile down the hallway
   to Mary's room where I sleep. & past the attic door? Past the empty
      room full of Kate's dolls' empty eyes & full of pony tails

made from her friend's hair dipped in wax? The room where she showed
   me the pictures she drew for her story about the girl who eats human
      beans for dinner? She told me the teacher

loved the story at her Catholic school. She said the big red A proved it.
   But she couldn't go back, cause nobody would admit that they liked it,
      even when she told them she made it up.

I wonder if that's why she's gone away now? Cause my dad said she
   doesn't work, said none of us work. I can still hear the song the girl
      sings to the beans in Kate's story,

I'm going to eat you for supper — & the song way back there down the hall
   on the radio. I can hear it from here. It's too far to go turn it off.
      & past the attic door & Kate's empty room? Once

in the daytime I went in the attic, just halfway up the stairs, & I went
   in Kate's room & saw a scary, stringy, bloody, sticky picture
      on the back of an album cover that I can't put down

or out of my eyes when they're closed. I listen to the Jackson Five
   by myself. They're from Gary. When I was little we drove to Florida.
      Kate said she saw the Jackson Five in a car

on the highway. They had a station wagon like ours. I remember,
   in Indiana, I began to count out loud to a million to get ready for school.
      I remember, in Georgia, everyone shouting,

& then clapping when I went in a pop bottle while we drove. It was hot
   in Georgia. I know all the Jackson Five's names & I know Michael wants
      to move mountains. But I don't know why?

Arms folded, he holds a flower between his fingers on my album
   cover. It's too far. & the woman's singing, sounds like what I heard
      Mary say about *Carrie*. I think she

goes to school with her. I listen at dinner when everyone talks about
   school. At school you have to know everything. But the teachers don't.
      Then I'm alone again at the table with my cold

squash. I want to help with dishes. Mary tells me by the time I'm tall enough,
   I won't want to anymore. Last year, mom "substituted"
      at school once. I know the word by heart

but like "exit" it's strange & I don't know what it means. She
   brought me home the most triangular paper airplane I'd ever seen.
      I try to match the folds, but mine don't

turn out. No matter what I do, I still hear the dying woman's song,
   it lasts for hours, it's longer than *Night Gallery*. It lasts all night.
      They won't turn it off for me, they won't come

up here, unless I tell them I need to go. & when I do that I have to act
   sleepy. They come for that, they remember what I did in the show
      window at the hardware store. Usually they

don't tell anybody else. It wouldn't flush. Sometimes when I think it might
    come up while they talk, I get a tight stomach & I think I can feel
        what a secret means. & what's so good

about them. In the Catholic church one day, when I was little, I remember
    the man said fathers should be home with their families. & he said secrets
        were evil. I wanted to raise my hand. I didn't.

I think that's why we don't go back anymore. People on TV die quick
    & wild like acrobats, they tumble like gymnasts. SWAT & Starsky
        & Fred, the talking parrot & Rooster's eye

on the sparrow *don't do the crime if you can't do the time*—The string sounds make
    the song float like a bird. A hawk or crow maybe, not a sparrow.
        Or like my airplane. In the song on the radio,

the woman sings about death but she doesn't shout or fall. She sounds
    alone. I'm afraid cause I'm the youngest & they'll take me & bury
        me in a coffin like that girl on TV

with a picture of my mom & a light. I saw it on my late night. They said
    it was a true story. I wonder if the soft-voiced dying lady's the youngest.
        Maybe her husband works. Or maybe he's

in Vietnam like my mom's friend's who's a librarian. I know her son. He's
    older than me. I didn't ask, but he tells me he doesn't miss his dad. I never
        thought of that. He says it real loud. I don't

know if I miss my dad who works. I don't think I would tell people loud
    if I did. Maybe I'd be quiet like the dying lady in the song. Maybe
        the dying lady & I are afraid of the same man:

the man with the hat & the black suit, who waits for me in my sleep, & says
    "gotcha" when I pull back the curtains. & the softly man that makes me
        think of the way my breath smells

on the window, when it rains at night in the summer. Kelly, the librarian's
son says his dad was a pilot. I show him my paper airplane. He says no,
that's an F-4. But I think it's a red A.

I lied. I told him I made it. I don't think he cared. He said no. His dad flew
in "helicopters." I asked if you had to know "helicopters" when you got
to school? He said he hates

school. Then, he began to stare at the ceiling light & spin around. While
our moms talked in the other room, he stretched out his arms
& made the sound.

Lights Out

He saved my soul from burning;
said he would, said he would
—Mahalia Jackson, "He Calmed the Ocean"

Close that book & read
   from peels of birch bark & sap
      hiss in the fire.

Whip pops as flames cut
   my cheeks, reveal red
      sandstone

beneath my skin. Sweat-visions,
   a sidewinder on its back,
      glowing

smoke-grey shards land
   on my bare belly. Quick get
      the shell

& put your ear down. Hear
   my skinned sea boil. Tattoos?
      Too nasal,

like playing "Harmonique" on blades
   of grass between fingers
      or on comb

& tissue. Go on & *graze at the edges*
   but stop after that page
      of Whitman.

Bee stings are in the ballpark.
   Wood burners give in
      to intent,

might as well go write your name
   in the snow. Sit ups are far
      too vague,

that shallow ache could mean
   just about anything. It has no edge
      or past.

& like sweat off fake sex, it's gone
   soon as you stop with all the
      pageantry

& writhing *I'll huff & I'll puff*—
   now a piece of broken
      mirror

can get you going. But exercise
   leaves no lasting scars
      to work with.

Might as well sit by the door
   & beg advice of fleas. Here now,
      your eyes close

down tight as frayed slip knots
   & fingers read my raw flesh.
      A pulse rises

in Braille. Dry lips mouth words,
   or count spades, in blistered
      scales.

1955

Ask Prof Smith or the bartenders
   at The Barley Duke. He taught me to shave
      & they know it's never done

with mirrors. On some nights, I slip off in a swirl.
   Parabolas slice the night from the silent
      web like boomerangs. Scales arc

in a calculus of windblown ribbons dipped
   in indigo. I count time three tempos at once
      & call new phrases like a table

of African gents I saw dropping ayo beans
   & insult-math into mahogany bowls
      at Café de la Paix.

That's when I'll play whatever & whoever falls
   beneath my hands. You could be my next song
      but I'm not the flurry of a man

you'd imagine with a gold eyetooth & mother
   of pearl fingerprints. Lately, I can't sleep.
      Surrounded by radiator clangs

& neon buzz from the window, when I close
   my eyes you breathe in red air & sit down topless
      at the edge of the bed. You spit cherry

pits on the floor & roll a full nipple slowly
   like a ripe date between your octave-thumb
      & index finger. Leaning

over, your shadow covers my face. You lick
   your thumb & ask difficult questions
      about where I am.

{

It's a year this week. All the trouble
    started when my shut eyes wouldn't sleep.
        & then last night I lost

my reflection to the puddle outside
    Birdland. Damn what I said they should
        have known what I meant.

& when they began to play, even the insomniacs
    heard the changes gone coming in Pree's last breath.
        Everyone saw her walk into the room.

But from there I'd have to go back. With
    a hayseed sounding country girl & the pale
        wink of an Ozark half moon

on her belly as my witness, it took all summer
    in the woodshed with a stack of Basie records
        before I thought I knew

what it was I heard. By then, somnambulist
    in an eleven year panic quoting Klosé at Lucia's Paradise,
        I'd begun to experiment with rhythm

words & a few other good reasons for narcolepsy.
    I put whetstone to the night's edge & stashed
        full blown mornings, dreams of catgut,

& Achilles' dime-works from the KCPD in rotten
    stumps & hollow tree trunks of Paseo Park. Played
        jobs for Tutty, stuck between

a goat named T. J. P. & a parrot that chanted, "bwak!
    nigger," in my ear. One night, head full of my mother's
        tonic, I caught an officer

down on his luck. He bit a hole in his lip & tried not
    to bob his head. I snuck a quote of "Precious
        Lord" into "Don't Blame Me."

{

Within months, in one solo phrase
    I could summon snakes out of chili bowls
        or McShann tunes & call out

Ben Webster, sweat dripping eavesdrops
    on blurry note cards, in a dark corner
        of the Savoy. But even in LA,

I couldn't never get Maggie to say *Le Sacre*
    du Printemps with a straight face. Wide open
        tattooed on lids, my eyes peer

inward. Anyone knows not to wake up
    a sleepwalker on stage in stocking feet
        blowing a boxcar up hill

to Chicago. Even full of fresh Spring breeze
    like Marcel Mule blowing Julia Wright's
        toy sailboat across the pond

at Le Jardin de Luxemburg, I kept one eye
    on the guy with the coke bottles at the Paradise
        Ballroom in Detroit.

At the Pershing in Chicago, the crowd entranced,
    I saw Dizzy smile & couples began to move
        with waves in the air.

Pendulum hips swayed & hums joined scarlet
    shades of a new moon to the missing ace
        in an uncalled hand.

≀

Now, I can't get a wink. My reflection's
    still in the puddle outside the club
        & they won't let me in

without it. That stage is no place
    for these slippers & I can't shake the dead
        taste in my mouth. Born

out of a crack in a Kansas sidewalk, Ikey & I left
    Sumner & crossed the river. We saw dry stone sprout
        lilac & juniper before we knew

what a half brother was. Before I could read, I'd
    dreamt the smell of burning leaves as pollen drops
        on a spotted fawn's

nose & knew the dust kicked in my eye
    was the cold riddle of the Milky Way. Give me
        a date with ribeca, I'll tear

open a ballad to where you don't know what
    love is, or if you've kissed your grandmother
        goodnight or ridden

an ex-lover bare back thru the room moaning
    like Rubberlegs Williams crossed up by
        two sips of my Café Bennie.

I kissed Tadd myself on "Lady Be Good."
    & on "Yatag" my one & only voice could glow
        like angel wings in Paradise.

Give me six months at the Beaux Arts in Paris.
I'll make your hands sweat. I'll make you blush
in church & apologize to strangers.

‹

Don't call it bop. & never ask Mr. Robeson
   if he's thirsty before a show. Only Walter knows
      what price love

by my heart, not strung tight as a viola in Monk's
   worn out copy of Berg's "Allegro Misterioso."
      I'm floating off

holding the anchor & people call me heavy.
   Could have kissed my card goodbye, in a nightmare,
      I left M.L. & O.G.

on a torn napkin, flipped a table, & stalked my
   shadow out of the 2nd Avenue Deli. Back
      in the street, a blast

of north wind slips under my shirttail & I'm
   steaming like a teapot in an icebox. That
      night I slept on a borrowed

clarinet chez Bellevue. Could have sworn
   it was Tunis at dawn & I saw a Marabout
      put lips to a black turtle.

Instead, he stood waist deep in the Ganges
   at Varanasi & chanted ancient patterns
      over intricate slices

in the sinners' immortal flesh. Then I heard Lily
   Pons in the slumped back & guttural
      hum. He turned,

motioned to a gray squall of voices, & blessed
   an upturned shell filled with bloody
      chunks of Sacrament.

§

Call me Charlie Chan.
   Let's pretend you know me
     from Oxford, & don't

drop bags of powdered tears in my coat
   pocket. More like the palm of my hand
     than anything

I ever heard these streets whisper
   to little boys. Now I want
     to say, "stick with me

kid, I'll show you how to turn
   a blues velvet side in, clear out
     the Open Door

with a couple hicks singing 'Route 66,'
   play a solo set hot as a shot of flaming
     Bourbon at

The Savannah Club, & still make
   yourself sixty bucks from the second
     seating across the street.

This here's the Scrappled Apple
   & you better believe every day's Halloween.
     Hand slaps & entropic

hustles won't get you back to New
   Hope or onto any wet-dream
     bandstand." Now I say,

"let's go to the bridge with The Salvation
Army brass, get on the rail, & play
the Join Hands Jump."

{

You just can't walk away from a face
    like Mrs. Berg. Tonight, my name bleems
      in the sky

over the valet's shoulder as Nica
    arrives hooded in a cashmere cape.
      A silver-lined

funnel cloud floats out of a limousine
    & over a puddle in the street.
      My vision split

open by hollow fangs or forks of lightning;
    it's the first five minutes of sleep
      I've had in months.

Like the black diamond of a timber rattler
    from an underbrush lair, or blue bolts
      out of yellow eyes

in a benighted sky, they strike before you see
    the flash. Hard to catch a real breath
      in the whiteness

of this spot before thunder claps leap
    out of charred voids left by silk sheaths
      for mute thighs.

Even in double time & off skyscrapers,
    "three Mississippi" means I must be uptown
      when a Chanel spike

pierces my liquid cheek. I feel a phantom
   touch from Robert's hand & I'm deaf at last
      to echoes of Diz

on the mic at the Deuces. In the way rain begins,
   the image slips beyond solace & I tremble
      with "Embraceable You."

More Here Than Gone

A red velvet arm
   reaches off a chair. Without
     aches & sighs

of habit, maple curves lose
   their shape, kinship to secret
     bends

in the family. An elbow's cradle
   held a baby girl. The curve
     in my sister's

back. A faint tambouritsa
   rhythm, a cloud of home
     in a pickup

that smells of tar dust
   & cigar ash. On blushed hips
     of a cushion

rests the cheek of a lover
   that never made the family name.
     Who lived

in an uncle's workday, between intuition
   in a wood rasp & photographic
     contours

in his palm. Smooths the tremble
   in a final polish, the grain moves
     under

his hand. A name whispered
   into a sunrise & curtains nod
     in the south

breeze. Leans against the swayed back,
   a hand appears too soft to brush
      his throat.

False Ceilings

In a sky full of people—
—Seal

We punched thru & found
  Transbluency above our heads
    plaster dust

from the archway   new born fornix
  of the missing room   dry mist in silken
    spirals   gesso

falls away like a silver lynx from
  bare shoulders   ripple-cloud   cream
    into coffee   heavy

aroma from a frost bouquet
  at the window   inhales
    cool as lighter

fluid & breath burns celestial
  burns a tektite cyclops
    eye   opens

into leaded feathers
  etched in a fine beveled
    pane

᠑

Outside   a night flurry & an upturned
  sky   a gelid paper dome   origami
    an obsidian swan

swims an infinite pond   parallax
  & purdah   until scarlet
    glow rounds

the rim   elbow gloves & brass
  opera glasses peer from the balcony
    at Adelphi

a beat farmer moonlights in Saratoga
  Springs   1841   plays fiddler to blackbirders
    hawk-eyes tangle

in his hair   dawn leaves a faint scent
  of poteen & a frayed hem
    in the sky's mufti

≀

White dust on red ribbons   kowtow
 & midnight veil to black ice on a switchback
  clean blade & crushed bone

powder from a mammoth tusk   new wind
 & the sidewinder crest of a Mojave
  dune   triangulated geographies

flesh toned & astronomical   keen specks   mute
 impulse & bent reeds   screech & silent
  jetsam

an infrared bend in Lethe   just another ultraviolet
 catastrophe   & memories in pidgin   night rain
  in mooneyes   redshift

& lightning on the cornea   shanghaied
 in Kingston   sold by the tael   a silversmith's
  lump weighed

against a fourth dimension   rhythm
 in waves   memento of salt
  vein &
     flota

＞

A dead cat on a quantum line
　　in the sky　hours until a Mohawk
　　　　tracker's dawn

We're awakened & called out into it　before
　　flakes grow designs & sleeted
　　　　purposes return

before bora unleash the cold facts
　　tear thru cheeks　make teeth
　　　　ache　catch still

winds　counterpoise & off balance　not
　　yet brittle　yet not sable　an instant
　　　　& cloudless sky

snows with no regard for whitefall or gravity
　　bits of star bristle & nonchalance
　　　　Scorpio?　or a bent

fork missing a prong　a sterling promise
　　pounded flat　chicken down
　　　　on a blood stained

anvil dusted blue　a silver band left behind
　　a silent fold added to Maryland's
　　　　border on midnight

≀

Ghosts breathe this kind of stillness
   running faster along the
     riverbank

a neck on nevernever   unmoored
   to sounds of wispthump
     & diastole's

allegro   knees quickened by pea sprouts
   sewn into the skin   upstream
     ice banks arch

& buckle   a full moon's weight
   on the
             surface

᠔

Flake & wink to nose tips   or melt
   by breath drawn from
      a night of wings

broken   & fallen like white
   there are still spots   missing from
      these woods   still

empty rooms overhead   full of touch-tones
   & ditches dug by turns of phrase
      horses still

won't cross   shared breaths cleared dark paths
   thru nightchants sharp as diamond dust in candlelight
      lullabies of mint leaf

& slow burn   murmur & whiskey rub
   on newborn gums   silent songs
      turned hip-deep

in mud into slip-streams of onomatopoeia
   in rivers of last-ditch & catch-can
      time rushes

over earthen roots   cypress & poplar
   bore down   torn between heat
      at the center

& wet at the edges   sodden veins twist
   & pulse in the forest's memory   smooth braids
      of beatitude

& vengeance   a God-father named
   for white tooth & mouthflash   smoke
      into a night

that lasted three days   left a trail
   none followed   an aftertaste of gunpowder
      turned into thunder

⸮

Breath clouds rise from the bank
   frozen & rhythmical   footfalls vanish
     into swishpat

systole's brushes on the snare   hand in hush
   in hand in   hush in hand   counter-
     balance   syzygy

& the Magi   unio mystica & a lift in the cold
   chains turn nickel back into moonlight
     gyves fall away

smoke rings blown from ash wrists
   or step   into circles of talc figures
     buried in burlap

sacks filled with red pepper
   & dog hair   they never recovered
     the bodies   so

it was a lift   then   windswept & metabolic
   gossamer   of unbreakable
     blue

Karmen

in a Clarke mood, hums spirals of jasmine.
  Just noses & ear lobes in dim fleeting zones
    & gray peculiar paths.

Smoke wonders along her leg. Learns
  her. She travels past nonchalance, risen
    in a tumbling room.

Ends lightly sanded, diamond thief fingers see her way
  beyond her reach. A third floor cantor calls her shadow
    thru the air-shaft. Eyes shut

she follows. Tulips & tongue tips trace shapes, drum invisible
  combos. She plays the great bassists. They leave
    her arched

& numb, with no earth between her moments.
  Grown up nimbus in pitch green scent of myrrh,
    storms of her approach.

Breath billows dark & about to pour down,
  or linger in silent clouds of heat lightning. Distant amber
    behind her head,

a schizophonic quiet storm fades in Minnie
  Riperton inhales to hold Hathaway exhales
    blown in cold gusts.

Still tremors recede. Coiled in deadly pose, when her fever
  breaks she'll shed screams in gallons. For each layer in scales,
    shed in Aztec scar patterns.

Isatine Blues

"Why? It don't matter why."
—*Billie Holiday, "Deep Song"*

Don't sing it
   to me. Or I'll stay under
      here motionless

& blue-gilled. I'll drift
   away from the shattered place
      of irruption.

Where the summer song
   crossed the winter street,
      the corner

where we met. & don't
   worry about me,
      I'll stick close

to pockets of air beneath
   the surface. Snatch shallow
      breaths of marrow

from bends in the death-blue
   shoulder blade of the ice patch.
      Go on & sing it,

just not to me. Last night,
   for a moment at rest
      on the keys,

I saw my finger tips melt
   chord prints into your frozen
      back. & Gershwin's

limo didn't come around
   to keep us honest. As you
      hummed changes

thru the tune the pockets
   of touch filled with water.
      & scarred

by warmth, they freeze again
   into glassy bullet wounds
      like transparent

Braille domes. My fingers
   slip off rounded keys;
      singularist,

I lose hold of you.
   & another song's gone
      off with the pale

frigoric voice, alight
   with the lilt of Southern
      flame.

Am I playing a player-
   piano? Behind the stool,
      a white veil wafts

as a bowl full of tangerine
   peels dries on a hissing radiator.
      Ancestress to burnt

lips on a scarlet trumpet,
   you turn body heat into liquid
      distance & back

to ice beneath my hands.
   Almost round, a charcoal sketch
      of a circle, we

dance underneath the ice,
   impaled by bolts of broken
      moonlight

& swayed in the tidal pull
   of silence. Sing to me now,
      rallentando down

to the sine qua non. Sing
   to me again & all last night.
      & don't pause

at my fall away thru
   scented pillows & cloudless
      depths of the

sheets. Confess it
   this once, the uncanny
      chance.

The whetstone in your pocket
   & the unsheathed épée
      waved in your

voice. I stayed alert,
   but my whole body fell
      asleep. Round

about midnight & crescendo
   needles hold my limbs.
      Sing my forehead

back thru the eye
   of the needle or a
      millionth

of the mirror. Been under
   five minutes now, lungs ache
      & clutch, ears

drum a pressure rhythm
   to the echo-depth of time.
      If you're down,

stay down. & sing me back
   thru last night before I went
      touch-deaf

& ear-numb, before I melted
   at the edge of your lips
      & slipped beneath

the sand. & don't stop. Quiver-
   still, how the hands of a mesmerist
      work the future

out of fruit fallen from the Litchi
   tree. When you hum
      lightning

into Mera's "Higanbana,"
   a blue tree at the river bank burns
      orange, blown

in a red wind. Our storm tongues
   twist Madame Butterfly
      onto her mythic

back & summon a thunder-reaper
   with a Cutthroat on his
      shoulder. A mirror

image or a sure sign, a raven
  wears a ruby necklace,
    Amadina fasciata.

Splayed open down to our beating
  pit, two well ripened sinners
    washed up

onto broken glass & black coral
  of the soul's beach. I'm hanging
    on one muted line,

to touch the indigo heave
  of nightfall to the windward
    surf of cachexy. ·

If tone is homage to the pressure
  of secrets, sing to the numb
    spot, the nob

of bone growing behind my ear.
  Sing the warm spot that moves
    along my hip.

Spheres

—after Monk

a brand burned into naked wood   Property of PS 129
  an old-time upright wheeled out to the playground
    paradiddle & round the back   hand clap

& tight coil rhythm bounce   eyes closed   smoke stained
  finger tips tangent to ivory   sunshine in a wide-open mouth
    light poured like syrup   fast twitch reflex & cold

      trust   an amber lyric   between blurry
      strangers

§

a 3d compass swipe   bloom & dance of exactitude
  theory & practice of minimal periphery   chords aclang
    how to eat sound with chopsticks   echoes in a Spalding

deity of content   criss-cross & nylon   played out on bent words   an orb
  cradled in a swan wrist   a drop in the bucket   wrist flick &
    arc   Pivot & tango with gravity   outside the

    fence   fish out of water

⟨

a calm afternoon sea   dark with oblique sunrays
   a pack of bluefish & a school of herring   frenzy & every
     splash aflame   every ripple a molten

sneer   gulls hover & dive   seize specks of flesh
   & soar   tiny drips of metal spin & fall
     into lighted crystal lips

      of the stone

≷

at 16   switch ends   & talk the new
    stuff   you follow   if I trace a circle on the court   say
        6 inches around

& now I trace the same circle   circumference 6   on this here
    ball   the radius on the ball   is shorter   like you
        shorter   than the one on the ground

forget what he says   check

⌇

smooth creme & scarred-over   broken scales   back
  cuts & passes snap   vector & no look witness to a path
  on the sharp rim of blueing   optimal

route   some say   between A & B   leaves no puncture
  no mark on the skin   travels a surface of unlimited size
  pulse & translucent gourd to the

    smallest possible
          infinite space

Guerilla Calligraphy

Midnight, I blow across your open lips to find the hollow call
    of a dry ceramic jug. Empty again, you're the first boy
        I ever

met. I was 20 before I saw these mud banks take on flesh
    & grow red hair at dawn. Now, in August,
        saw grass stirs

agnosia into tableaux vivants. No more braided rain baskets
    on the 19th green. Our childhood's gone condo
        & I dreamt that grass still

grows luminescent & razor sharp, windward leaves of a night-stalker's
    karma. New South or Up South, you're the same to me: 9 years
        old & chasing us off the playground,

a cat by the tail, hellbent & swinging like a whirligig; or as an altar
    boy at 16, head bowed & aglow with candle eyes. Part twin
        brother or a pen-name,

clouded mirror or surrogate father. When he re-upped & left,
    you missed not a beat with pet names & designs for the bedtime
        underside of my flamethrower's

eyelids. Early hours at the public library checking every card
    between Viet-minh & Vinh d'alho. Cross-referenced indexes
        & stashing sub-tropical botany

under the geographical rug. If I stopped by you'd be quick,
    let's play vingt-et-un & the thin military paper threw us all for a
        minute. But who could mistake

a 13 year old Chattanoogan's skyfuls of air strikes & palmfuls
    of foxfire conjured from somewhere between gutturals on CBS News
        at Six & the way moonlight stings

a willow on a vacant playground. I read every night. & never
  thought about what that war sent to me. Letters addressed to Rani,
    but written to me, were all I had

to go on. I was 25 when mom died & they handed me the truth bound
  with string in a shoe box. My father's real letters made me
    anonymous, like anyone

who plays with mirrors & glimpses her face braided tight from behind.
  I saw a stranger's eyes sway overhead from monsoon drenched jute
    bridges that always joined nowhere

to somewhere in your version of the story. The bridges unravel,
  ground us in takeoff. What else attaches earth to the first moments
    of sleep? & so what

if I owe you Silly Putty tattoos, those Faustian tremors, & still hold fast
  to the last breath & full stop in each bead of sweat? If you can't get over
    the rhythm of the delta,

then the surface of the summer wind will be our ceiling. & we'll roll
  with oceans overhead, covered by night flown sheets
    of virga. We'll carve an X

on the bank with sticks & slice open the one moment between here
  & there. The storm nears, we hear earlobe whispers brush up.
    That's us, hard-shucked

& soft as silk from sweet corn. Mine's the voice you don't hear by itself,
  with these hands, echoes cover your ears. We spin in cyclones of Victrola
    visions, Wingy Manone & the Lady, a one-arm

rower & the snake-bit charmer. Pounded thin, the left side's sound
  asleep. Beyond the lyric raphe over your shoulder, this river takes my arm
    into its silver sleeve of needles.

Ed Pavlić is a graduate of the University of Wisconsin-Madison and Indiana University. He currently teaches in the English Department of Union College. His critical and creative work has appeared in journals such as *African American Review, Black Warrior Review, Colorado Review,* and *DoubleTake.* His critical book, *Crossroads Modernism,* is forthcoming in 2002 from the University of Minnesota Press. He lives in Schenectady, New York, with his wife Stacey, son Milan, and daughter Sunčana.